Get Started.

Start and grow a profitable business. A quick-start guide for entrepreneurs who want to work from home

CATHERINE MAYOKUN EGWALI

https://catherineegwali.com

ISBN-13: 978-1984180261
ISBN-10: 1984180266

DISCLAIMER

This book and the items it distributes contain strategies, methods and other advice that, regardless of my own results and experience, may not produce the same results (or any results) for you. Catherine Mayokun Egwali makes absolutely no guarantee, expressed or implied, that by following the advice or content available from this book or provided by Catherine Mayokun Egwali, you will get free training opportunities, save any money or improve current status, as there are several factors and variables that come into play regarding any given undertaking.

Primarily, results will depend on the mindset you have, nature of the business you are in, career path chosen, the conditions of your environment, the experience of the individual, and situations and elements that are beyond your control.

As with any endeavour in life, you assume all risk related to investment and money based on your own discretion and at your own potential expense.

URGENT PLEA!

Thank you for reading this book.

If you have found this book useful, I would really love to get your feedback and know how this book has impacted your life.

It would greatly help me to make the next version better.

Kindly leave a helpful review on Amazon letting me know your thoughts about this book!

Many thanks. I really appreciate your time and effort.

Catherine Mayokun Egwali

DEDICATION

This book is dedicated all stay at home moms, work from home moms, and all entrepreneurs who are determined to add value to their world by doing a business they enjoy

CONTENTS

ACKNOWLEDGMENTS

I give all thanks to God almighty for the opportunity to write this book.

1 INTRODUCTION

If you will like to start a business that is rewarding and beneficial, this book is for you!

I wrote this book to guide others who desire to start a profitable online business so they can make impact, add value and make money. It contains strategies I have learnt over time to build a profitable online business. Fortunately for you, you do not have to spend years of what business to start. I have gone through the trial and error stages and have compiled what works in this book so that you can get started with your business easily and quickly.

It is possible to succeed and grow a legitimate business online.

I know it is because I and many others have done it. I believe you too can succeed.

I know you will succeed as long as you put to work the knowledge gained from the contents of this book.

Success is yours as long as you work at it. Go succeed because the world is waiting for your solutions!

2 BRAINSTORMING BUSINESS IDEAS

You have decided to start an online business. You have written out your reasons for being in business. You have the basic tools needed to get started. Now the question is, what should you do to earn some income? In today post, we will be reviewing how to go about generating ideas for businesses you can dabble into so you can start profiting from your business.

There are several ways to decide on what business to start. However, today's task will help lay a foundation for making the right choice.

Ideas on what you CAN do to start an online business

1. WHAT ARE YOU GOOD AT?
Can you speak your native language fluently? Are you good at dancing, singing, identifying when someone is unhappy? Can you repair electronic devices even though you didn't receive formal training for it?

2. WHAT SKILLS DO YOU HAVE?
Do you know how to manage money well i.e. good at budgeting and financial management? Do you know how to teach toddlers and have them understand? Do you have website or graphic design skills?

3. WHAT HAVE YOU DONE IN THE PAST – INFORMAL WORK?
For example you might have ran some errands for people, you might have helped to babysit your cousin when you went to spend the holidays at your aunt's, you might have sold items to your classmates while in school.

4. WHAT JOB ROLES HAVE YOU HELD IN THE PAST?

Have you worked as a sales executive before? Perhaps you have held a job role as a front desk officer to welcome visitors? Whatever job roles you have held in the past be it as an IT officer, Support engineer, HR personnel, you can note them down.

5. WHAT DO YOU ENJOY DOING?

Some people love to wash clothes. Do you enjoying watching movies? Some people love to go shopping. For example I love to shop and to watch movies. Or perhaps you enjoy organising parties? Whatever you enjoy doing, note them all down.

6. WHAT BOTHERS YOU WHEN YOU SEE OTHERS DO IT WRONGLY? ARE THERE THINGS YOU SEE DONE AND FEEL COULD BE BETTER CARRIED OUT?

Note them down. You might be able to create a better solution that people will find appealing.

7. WHAT KNOWLEDGE DO YOU HAVE AS A RESULT OF TRAINING OR SCHOOLING?

For example, you might know how to treat wounds because you are a trained nurse. You might know how to repair electronics because you were taught in the technical school you attended. You might know how to handle book keeping because you are a trained accountant. List out the knowledge you have that might be of benefit to others.

8. WHAT HAVE YOU LEARNT TO DO BY YOURSELF SUCH THAT YOU HAVE BECOME QUITE GOOD IN IT?

Some people are very good at playing video games. They have learnt some tricks and hacks that give them an upper edge each time they play. Are you one of such people?

9. WHAT KNOWLEDGE HAVE YOU GAINED BY VIRTUE OF YOUR ASSOCIATION TO A GROUP, FAMILY OR CLUB?

It could be a special baking recipe that has been passed down the years to you by your great grandmother. It might be even be new knowledge gained from being a part of a Facebook group, church, or a network marketing group.

10. WHAT CHALLENGES OR FAILURES IN YOUR LIFE HAVE YOU OVERCOME AND CAN TEACH TO OTHERS?

Some people have survived traumatic experiences and can now help others overcome similar experiences. For example, if you have learnt how to lose weight and maintain a slim figure, you can help other do the same.

11. WHAT ABILITIES COME NATURALLY TO YOU SUCH THAT YOU TAKE THEM FOR GRANTED?

Do you know how to persuade people to do almost anything you want them to? Perhaps you can tell when someone is unhappy regardless of if the person is laughing or not. Whatever comes like second nature to you but may not be so natural to other people should be written down. You might be able to profit from your unique abilities.

Did you know that you can watch movies and blog about them? Such a site can end up being a high traffic site if people enjoy your style of writing and the reviews you give. You can choose to monetise such a site via advertising. You may even get paid by producers who desire you review their movies as it could lead to increased sales for them.

Do you see how all these tie up? Hence do not miss writing down whatever comes to mind as an answer. You would be surprised to find out that you can monetise your experiences and make a fortune from them.

A way to answer some of the questions above is to look inward and do some self-discovery sessions.

Write down your answers in your book as the thoughts come to your mind. You may even ask other people for their opinions.

What do you think of the methods above?

Have you tried any of the methods above to generate business ideas before?

Write down the ideas within a book or use our complementary journal to note down your answers.

3 IDENTIFY A NICHE/MARKET TO ENTER

Now that you have written down things you can do, teach or help people with, you need to determine what business you should invest your time and resources in.

There are 3 main niches/markets that are profitable when considering an online business.

They are
1. Relationship niche (Marriage, Dating, Parenting, Divorce, Love etc)
2. Money and wealth niche (Real estate, Investing, Sales, Marketing, Financial management, Online business etc)
3. Health, fitness and wholeness niche (Weight loss, Supplements, Nutrition, Diet, Exercise etc)

The niches above are broad categories having sub-niches, some of which are listed in bracket beside them. Group your ideas under the niches above and identify your sub-niche/create a sub-niche if necessary. Your objective is to consider business ideas that belong to sub-niches that are profitable, not saturated and in great demand.

For example you can have this sub-niche:
 Wealth niche > Online Business > Lead generation via LinkedIn advertising

4 DETERMINE THE BUSINESS TO INVEST RESOURCES IN

If you have identified a niche/market to operate in, you need to consider some factors before investing all your resources in your new business.

PROPERLY ANALYSE YOUR TARGET MARKET

Do not start a business just because you know how to do the business. Ensure there are enough people in your target market who would want to buy from you. Most importantly, ensure you can identify who your ideal customers are and how to sell to them.

I can remember when I first started my business in the United Kingdom. I wanted to start with Unified Communications (UC) and VOIP (Voice Over Internet Protocol) services. I had experience managing those services at my previous place of work so naturally, I was excited about selling them.

I already knew about identifying my target market. However, I did not do proper market segmentation nor create a persona of my ideal clients.

For the VOIP services, my target customers were Nigerians living in the Diaspora who would love to call people in Nigeria. My product entailed providing a Nigerian number that could be used from anywhere in the world, without roaming charges, as long as the user had access to the internet. Call charges were also at Nigerian landline rates. However, most people I spoke to preferred to buy calling cards or bundled call packages from telcos who gave cheaper rates. In the end, I had to focus on other services like website design and hosting as I got more people who were interested in those.

In retrospect, the UC and VOIP services did not take off as expected because I didn't analyse the market properly and I targeted the wrong people. If there is a market for your product/niche but you fail to consider factors like identifying your ideal customers, proper analysis of your target market, market segmentation etc your business will not last long.

FIND OUT IF PEOPLE ARE WILLING AND ABLE TO PAY

If you want to start an online business, it is important to know if your target customers in your niche are ABLE and WILLING to buy.

Russell Brunson, in his book "Expert Secrets", gave an illustration of his friend who had created a course to help people play video games better. However, his friend had targeted kids as his customers. It was after he had spent a fortune launching his product he discovered his mistake; his target customers did not have credit cards to make their purchase and that affected his business.

You do not have to make the same mistake. Do not spend a fortune launching your online business without ensuring your target customers are willing and able to pay.

SELL WHAT PEOPLE WANT TO BUY NOT NECESSARILY WHAT THEY NEED

Always think NOT ONLY in terms of what people NEED but also what THEY WANT.

This is a profound truth as confirmed by Akin Alabi in his book "Small Business, Big Money".

One of his students had created an Information Product on "How to obey traffic in Lagos. As much as it is great to obey traffic rules in Lagos, a lot of people will be more interested in knowing how to beat traffic rules to get to their destination on time.

Akin's opinion of the product was that it was not likely to be very successful except the product had the backing of the government, perhaps by forcing it on motorists. Why? The product is something people NEED but not what they WANT.

What do you think? If someone offered you the traffic product to buy, would you buy it? Be truthful to yourself and let me have your answer in the comment section.

DETERMINE DEMAND AND PROFITABILITY TO ENSURE THE SUSTAINABILITY OF YOUR BUSINESS

Do not go investing your time, money and other resources in a product or service if you have not validated that there is a strong market for it.

You are in business to make a profit. If you invest in a niche with low demand you won't last long in business. Ideally, you should be looking for a strong market itching to have the solutions you offer. You want to be sure of making a significant profit from your online business.

5 HOW TO IDENTIFY A PROFITABLE NICHE

Here are some ways to find out if your business idea/product/niche would be profitable:

1. Conduct market surveys to know if people would be interested in your product

2. Use Google search volume to get an idea of the number of searches for related products or ideas

3. Use Google trends to find out if the search trend for the idea/product/niche is stable, increasing or dying. You should be looking for evergreen niches that are still relevant.

4. Check if the product/niche has hundreds or thousands of reviews plus high search volume on Amazon

5. Look for products and merchants on affiliate platforms such as ShareASale etc. Profitable niches are usually those with a high number of sales with affiliates who make money from the sale of products in your desired niche.

Other methods as listed in Ronald Nzimora's "Sell Your Brain" book include

- Use Google Keyword Planner to check for high demand for your chosen sub-niche
- Use Forums like Nairaland to find out if people are interested in business ideas similar to yours. Do this by checking out the number of views and

replies on threads talking about similar business ideas to yours

- Use ClickBank Marketplace to gauge the popularity of products similar to yours or in the same niche as yours
- Find out if some competition exists for your product/business. Competition simply means buying customers exist and is a good sign that the niche is favourable.

Ensure you note down your findings in your book as you do your research. Review them and in the end, make your choice based on the factors revealed in this book.

6 CONCLUSION

This book shows you how to identify business ideas you can start so you can make money doing what you love or know to do.

In summary, carry out the following to get started with your next business project.

1. Ensure you identify the proper target customers for your niche,

2. Consider niches you have a passion for as it will help you weather business storms that might arise,

3. Confirm niche profitability and

4. Settle for a niche that is in high demand

ABOUT THE AUTHOR

Catherine Mayokun Egwali a #1 international best-selling author of The Competent Entrepreneur. She is also the co-founder of Switem Technology Solutions, a technology solutions company that helps business owners to solve problems and achieve their goals through the use of technology. She is also an ICT Business Consultant with several years of experience in the ICT industry.

In 2009, she was awarded the prestigious NYSC Presidential Honours award for her contribution to her nation during her national service year. During that period, she was involved in organising youth empowerment programs, ICT training, establishment of an ICT center for the community secondary school she served in, as well as other community development services.

She currently helps business owners to grow their competence, earn more money, and grow their business via technology solutions and the development of a competent entrepreneurial mindset. This has been observed to save them on business cost, earn an additional income and get results without being overworked, or losing out on forward-moving opportunities.

She is married and has a daughter. She also enjoys watching movies, shopping and traveling.

CONNECT WITH ME

Thank you so much for taking the time to read this book. If you would like to get in touch with me, feel free to contact me at https://catherineegwali.com/ . Alternatively, you can reach me at Switem Technology Solutions for ICT related solutions.

You can also connect with me on:

LinkedIn: https://www.linkedin.com/in/catherinemegwali/

Facebook: https://web.facebook.com/catherineegwali/

Facebook Group:
https://web.facebook.com/groups/ICTSavvyEntrepreneur/

Facebook Messenger Bot: https://m.me/catherinegwali/

Twitter: https://twitter.com/catherineegwali/

Instagram: https://www.instagram.com/catherineegwali/

BONUS

For buying a copy of my book, I will like to thank you by giving you a free 30-minutes Start Your Business clarity call session.

Ordinarily, this session costs $250 but I will be giving you for free to help you gain clarity on how to start your business.

You can sign up for the call session here:

https://calendly.com/catherineegwali/clarity-session/